NO MORE MISTAKES

NO MORE MISTAKES

JAMES R. SHERMAN

First Edition, November, 1987
Copyright © 1987 James R. Sherman
All Rights Reserved

Library of Congress Catalog Number
87-062216

International Standard Book Number
0-935538-08-9

Pathway Books
700 Parkview Terrace
Golden Valley, Minnesota 55416
(612) 377-1521

To: Eric and Margaret

CONTENTS

SECTION III
HOW TO AVOID MISTAKES

Know Where You're Going
Get The Facts
Build On Your Strengths
Set Priorities
Know What To Expect
Be Responsible
Minimize Your Risks
Think Positively
Overcome Fear
Position Yourself
Visualize
Appreciate Time
Develop A Game Plan
Know Where To Start
Do One Thing At A Time
Run To Daylight
Go Steadily Into The Wind
Know When To Quit
Keep A Journal
Avoid Guilt
Share With Others
Reward Yourself
Make Success A Habit
Care Enough To Do Your Very Best

SECTION IV
YOUR PLAN OF ACTION

INDEX

PREFACE

Is it really possible to be error-free?

Some people say there is no such thing as a mistake-free person. I believe it all depends on your attitude.

Every society develops a set of attitudes toward what is and what is not possible. And inevitably, these attitudes set limits on performance.

For generations, people had the attitude that no one could run a mile in less than four minutes. But in 1954, Roger Bannister crossed the finish line in 3 minutes 59.4 seconds. The barrier went down, people's attitudes changed, and several other runners promptly duplicated Bannister's feat.

Successful people who turn out error-free performances believe in what they're doing. They are always looking for an opportunity to grow and a chance to have an impact on their changing environment. Their optimistic attitudes thrive, in spite of seemingly insurmountable barriers.

Getting through a normal day without making mistakes is just as possible for them as climbing Mount Everest, flying solo across the Atlantic, hitting 60 home runs, or getting a perfect score in Olympic gymnastics.

Error-free performances are those in which ignorance and a "can't do" attitude are eliminated, and participants are encouraged to succeed.

Like most other people, I put a premium on performance. I get frustrated whenever I make a mistake, because I know I'm either going to have to live with lousy results, or I'm going to have to do something over again.

I don't like mistakes, and I don't like the way they mess up my life. It doesn't make any difference if I've locked my keys in my car or if I've lost an entire manuscript on my word processor. Mistakes drive me up the wall.

I finally figured out that the only way I was ever going to reach my desired level of success was to quit screwing up so much. I began to read everything I could get my hands on to find out why I was not meeting my performance standards. That led to a list of 16 different things that were causing me to make mistakes. Some were obvious, others surprised me. When I found out what was causing my mistakes, I started thinking up ways of avoiding them.

This led to 24 simple, straightforward techniques for getting through life without dropping the ball. By applying these techniques to my day-to-day activities, I eliminated a lot of dumb mistakes and got rid of a lot of frustration. I felt better and got more done. You can have the same results just by reading this book and applying the same techniques.

You might not eliminate all of your mistakes, because that's hard to do, even for pilots, neurosurgeons, and Olympic athletes. But if you have the right attitude and believe in what you're doing, you'll get rid of most of them, starting with the little nuisance mistakes that keep you tied down to low levels of performance. Once you've gotten rid of those little monsters, you can move up to the big mistakes that keep you from reaching your hoped-for level of success.

Does eliminating mistakes still sound too easy to believe? Why not turn the page and find out how easy it really is.

James R. Sherman, Ph.D.

INTRODUCTION

Who says you can't win 'em all? Just because you've made a mistake or two in the past doesn't mean you have to keep making them the rest of your life.

Think for a minute. You wouldn't put your life in the hands of a surgeon who thought mistakes were par for the course. You wouldn't turn your income taxes over to a C.P.A. who thought an error-free return was too much to ask. And you wouldn't take your car to a mechanic who thought screwups were part of the American way of life. If you've been expecting other people to do things right, then why not set the same standards for yourself?

Make up your mind right now that you're not going to make any more mistakes. Follow the advice of Leo Hauser, author of the book, *Five Steps To Success*. "Shoot for the moon," he said, "because even if you miss by a little bit, you'll still end up among the stars."

Like most occasional duffers, you know you could be doing better. But you're frustrated, because costly, irritating errors have kept you from even getting off the ground. You've had to do a lot of things over again, or you've had to settle for less than satisfactory results, and that bothers you.

For years you've wanted to be happy and successful, to be praised instead of criticized. You picked up this book because you thought now there was a good chance of pulling it off. You're obviously motivated, so it shouldn't be hard for you to change the way you do things. All you need are some simple, straightforward suggestions that will show you where the problems are and tell you how to move ahead.

1

Here's a proven program that will get you started on the right foot and help make your journey an easy one.

HOW TO DO IT

There are four basic steps to becoming error-free. Tackle them with enthusiasm and determination and you'll soon put the kibosh on troublesome mistakes. The first step is the most important because the other three can't really be completed without it.

1. Make a commitment to yourself and the rest of the world that from now on you're not going to make any more mistakes.
2. Find out what's causing your mistakes. Learn what you can do to prevent them.
3. Write down the specific steps you're going to take to avoid making the kind of mistakes that have plagued you in the past.
4. Decide on a definite plan of action and carry it out.

Pause for a moment and review the commitment you made in step number one. Do you really think you can do it, or do you still think it's impossible? Are you a Roger Bannister or one who always runs in the back of the pack?

The goal of this book is to get you to believe in yourself. If you're not ready to do that, then go back and work some more on step number one.

Attitude is the biggest part of success. That's why the first step is so important. Once you've made up your mind that you're capable of an error-free performance, you'll be over the first hurdle and well on your way to the finish line.

It isn't going to be easy, because the possibility of making a mistake will still exist. The only guaranteed way of avoiding mistakes is to say nothing, do nothing, and be nothing. So you have to do your very best in everything you do, even after you've committed yourself to being successful. Otherwise you'll keep on making mistakes just as surely as night follows day.

I'll ask you from time to time to stop reading and to write down some notes to yourself. Don't brush these suggestions aside. They're designed to help strengthen your commitment and make it easier to eliminate your mistakes.

Now that you've committed yourself to being error-free, it's time to introduce you to some common mistakes. The more you know about these little gremlins, the easier it will be to avoid them.

COMMON MISTAKES

You can make little mistakes, like taking a wrong turn, spilling your coffee, or locking your keys in your car. Or you can make big mistakes, like failing to file your income tax, driving while intoxicated, or losing your Captain Marvel decoder ring.

Some of the most common mistakes are those in which you do something you aren't supposed to do. You do the wrong thing at the right time or place, or the right thing at the wrong time or place. Those are called *errors of commission*.

Filing income tax returns (right thing) after the April 15 deadline (wrong time) is a common error of commission. So is running a stop sign while taking your driver's license exam.

On the other side of the coin are *errors of omission* in which you fail to do something that you should be doing, like forgetting to put the toilet seat down. (Or is it up?)

You can also make *trigger errors*, in which you accidently do something without knowing why you're doing it. Something in your mind triggers an action that you're not aware of. You intend to take a familiar route to a friend's house, but you're diverted for some reason. Before you know it, you're going in a different direction toward your office. Trigger errors usually take place when your mind is preoccupied.

Errors of intention are also very common. You intend to do something, but you make the mistake of doing it to the wrong person. Husbands and wives yell at each other or at their kids instead of yelling at things that got them mad in the first place; things like big bills, burnt meals, traffic jams, or dumb bureaucrats.

Motivated mishaps are done accidently-on-purpose. There is a hidden motive for screwing up and only the person who does it knows what it is. A little brother forgets to replace the toothpaste cap, knowing subconsciously that his big sister will have a fit when she discovers it.

Persistence errors are made when you stick to a bad decision even though the evidence suggests you're wrong.

Task fixation errors are the result of being so preoccupied with one task that you overlook others that you should be working on. A recent Eastern Airlines crash provides a tragic example of this kind of mistake. The plane smashed into a grove of trees because the crew was so busy trying to solve an oil leak that they forgot to watch their altitude.

Alternation errors are those you make when you keep changing your mind, even though the information you're using to make your decisions remains constant.

Short-term memory overloads are mistakes that are caused by too much data coming in all at once. You can't wade through it fast enough to find the important data you need to make good decisions.

Internal models. You try to act on the model that's in your memory bank even though it doesn't apply to the task at hand. It's like trying to drive an eighteen wheeler when your only experience has been with the family station wagon.

Absentminded slips occur when you're performing almost-automatic routines amid familiar surroundings and you're distracted by a diversion or preoccupation. It's like trying to fix dinner in a kitchen full of jabbering kids.

Place-losing errors occur when you're interrupted in an sequence of actions. You lose your place, and make a mistake when you try to get back to where you left off.

WHERE MISTAKES OCCUR

You can make mistakes like those listed above in almost any situation; in your job, marriage, college career, personal relationships, or while driving home on the freeway. Your mistakes can be as simple as breaking a dish or forgetting a dental appointment. Or they can be as serious as marrying the wrong person, failing to get through college, or lousing up your professional career.

Marriage. Choosing the wrong mate is the one mistake people think about the most. But marital mistakes can also occur in other areas, like those listed below.

1. sex
2. vacations

3. bringing up children
4. budgets and finances
5. resolution of arguments
6. relationships with in-laws
7. employment of both spouses
8. good or bad health of either spouse
9. activities, interests, and hobbies outside the home
10. relationships with neighbors, common friends, or friends of either spouse

Jobs/Careers. The two most common mistakes are staying with a job you hate or quitting a job you should hang on to. You can also make the mistake of getting involved in tasks that are beyond your level of competency.

College. You can choose the wrong college, wrong roommate, wrong program of study, or wrong part of the country. Or you can fall into some lousy study habits.

Personal Health. You can make several mistakes that effect your health. Foremost among these are smoking, drinking too much, eating too many of the wrong foods, or just trying to do things that your body can't handle.

Stop for a minute and think about any mistakes you might have made in your marriage, job, college career, or health habits. Try to remember if you did something you weren't supposed to do or if you forgot to do something you should have. Think about trigger errors, errors of intention, or any other errors that might have had painful results.

Turn to page 6 and write down the most significant mistakes that come to mind. Make a note after each one as to how it fouled up your aspirations for success. Maybe you lost a job. Or maybe a close, personal friend quit seeing you because of something you said or did. If you can think of any other disastrous outcomes, be sure to add them to your list.

This little exercise is not intended as a head-bashing. It's designed to give you a better perspective on what caused your mistakes and what you can do to avoid them in the future. Nobody is going to come to your door and demand an accounting for something you did in the third grade. So feel free to write down anything that comes to mind.

SIGNIFICANT MISTAKES I HAVE MADE
AND THEIR CONSEQUENCES

Write down mistakes that kept you from getting things you really wanted.

1. Mistake _____

_____

    Consequence _____

_____

2. Mistake _____

_____

    Consequence _____

_____

3. Mistake _____

_____

    Consequence _____

_____

4. Mistake _____

_____

    Consequence _____

_____

PEOPLE WHO MAKE MISTAKES

All mistakes are first-time mistakes and anyone can make one. But only a dunderhead will make the same mistake time after time after time.

The only ones who never make mistakes are dead people and politicians who are up for reelection.

The capacity for an occasional blunder is inseparable from the capacity to make things happen. The more you work at being successful, the more likely you are to make a mistake. That's why it's going to be hard to eliminate *all* of your mistakes. But you can get rid of most of them if you really work at it.

Mistakes are not confined to dumbbells. On Christopher Columbus's first voyage across the Atlantic, he thought he had landed in India. He called the area the West Indies and the natives Indians.

Remember the Edsel? The engineers at the Ford Motor Company thought it would be the car of the future. And when the DuPont Company introduced Corfam, a synthetic leather they had spent $100 million to develop, they said it would do for shoes what nylon did for stockings. Unfortunately, both the Edsel and Corfam turned out to be classic flops.

The first comedy record album to sell over 1 million copies was called "Radio Bloopers". It was issued in 1954 and featured a collection of miscues that went out over the radio waves.

If you want to see how intelligent people screw up on a regular basis, just read the news from our nation's capital.

THE CONSEQUENCE OF ERROR

Big mistakes make the headlines, but small, apparently minor mistakes can cause just as much mayhem. Here are some notable consequences.

Mistakes Are Expensive. The $18.5 million Mariner I space probe ended in disaster four minutes into the launch when the spacecraft crashed into the Atlantic Ocean. Someone left out a minus sign in the computer program that controlled the rocket.

Mistakes Are Physically Painful. Sticking your hand in an alligator's mouth really hurts.

Mistakes Are Emotionally Painful. Embarassment and failure, when repeated and sustained over long periods of time, can wipe out a person's confidence and self-esteem.

Mistakes Are A Waste of Time. You lose valuable time whenever you have to go back and do something over again. And once you've lost time, it's gone. You can never get it back.

Mistakes Are A Waste of Resources. Flunking out of college means a waste of tuition, books, transportation, and room and board, as well as a loss of self-esteem. Divorces are notoriously expensive. And the loss of a job is not only a waste of human resources, but a drain on society as a whole.

Mistakes Are Aggravating. Foul-ups of any kind can lead to frustration, anxiety, anger, and hostility.

Mistakes Are Regressive. With most mistakes, you have to step backwards and repeat something to get ahead.

Mistakes Are Insidious. Blunders have a gradual and cumulative effect. You make one, and unless you're careful, you'll probably make another that is related to the first.

Mistakes Are Destructive. Houses have been known to burn to the ground because someone forgot to unplug an appliance.

Mistakes Are Repressive. The mistakes of the people below you pull you down. And the mistakes of the people above you put a ceiling on your ability to grow.

Mistakes Are Irreversible. What is done is done. You can't undo a mistake, you can only help reduce the consequences.

In spite of all the bad things that can be said about mistakes, they do not make bad people. In some cases, they provide learning experiences that can lead to happy and successful outcomes.

LEARNING FROM MISTAKES

Learning from your mistakes is a healthy and necessary part of growth. Feeling guilty about them is unhealthy, because you waste a lot of energy feeling hurt, upset, and depressed about something you can no longer do anything about.

If you feel embarassed by your mistake, especially over a long period of time, it will shake your confidence, lower your self-esteem, and keep you from learning how to avoid future mistakes. So the first thing you should do after screwing up is restore your self-confidence. Forgive yourself. Then figure out how you're going to avoid making the same mistake another time.

There are two kinds of mistakes: contructive mistakes from which valuable lessons can be drawn and gut-wrenching washouts that are total losses.

Constructive mistakes provide an opportunity to gather and use new information. But you still have to take advantage of the opportunity and make a conscious effort to learn. It hurts when you whack your thumb with a hammer. To learn how to keep from clobbering your thumb a second time, you either have to get someone else to hold the nail, or you have to learn to hold it the right way.

Sometimes the only thing you learn is to not do the same thing over again. You don't learn much after you've locked your keys in your car for the umpteenth time. You knew before you did it how expensive it would be to break a window and get back in.

Learn something new after you goof up and you probably won't make the same mistake twice. Learn something new *before* you start on your task, and you'll reduce the chances of making a mistake to almost nothing.

If you make a mistake, make the most of it. If you're going to fall, fall forward.

ON DECK

Section II contains a list of 16 different things that cause people to screw up. Keep a pen and some paper handy as you go through the list and write down any causes you can think of that aren't included. The more information you can gather about your mistakes, the easier it'll be to wipe them out entirely.

Section III provides 24 simple, straightforward techniques for avoiding mistakes. Again, if you can think of any additional techniques that aren't among the ones discussed, and if they've worked for you in the past, feel free to add them to your list.

By the time you finish this book, you should have a pretty good idea of what causes your mistakes and what you have to do to avoid them.

Now that you've got your momentum up, turn the page and find out what's caused you to miss the boat so many times in the past.

COMMON CAUSES OF MISTAKES

Take a minute now before you dig into this section and turn to page 12. Write down what you think are some of the major causes of your mistakes. List things like stress, forgetfulness, invading armies, or anything else that comes to mind. Try to come up with at least a half-dozen causes. Then, as you go through this section, compare your list with the various causes that are presented in the next several pages.

By writing down the causes of your mistakes, and referring to your list from time to time while you're reading, you'll get a better understanding of why mistakes are made, and you'll be more inclined to think of ways of avoiding them in the future.

Don't worry about matching your causes one to one with the causes you find here. You might have some causes on your list that aren't in this book. And there might be some listed here that you've never even thought about.

Read the description of each cause carefully and pay particular attention to the examples that are given. Then turn your creative juices loose and see if you can come up with similar examples that you've been involved with.

You want to accomplish two important objectives by the time you finish this section. You want to know why people in general – and you in particular – tend to make mistakes. And you want to start thinking of ways of avoiding the mistakes that bother you the most.

Here's the first, and probably the most common cause of mistakes.

SOME MAJOR CAUSES OF MY MISTAKES

Write down what you think are major reasons for screwing up.

_____

_____

_____

_____

_____

_____

_____

_____

_____

_____

_____

_____

_____

_____

LACK OF KNOWLEDGE

People who don't know what they're doing run a very high risk of making a mistake. They can cut that risk significantly by taking the time to learn everything they can about their task.

Here's an example of how lack of knowledge can affect your chances of success.

Picture yourself trying to cross a fast-moving stream you know nothing about. You have to decide whether to cross it or stay where you are. At first glance, there is a high risk of drowning. But a closer look tells you that the stream is only 2 inches deep. That knowledge, if you use it, minimizes the risk of making a wrong choice.

If the stream was 3 feet deep, there would still be a risk, but less than you originally thought. If the stream was 12 feet deep, you would have to abandon your attempt and look for another crossing or run the risk of going under.

Lack of knowledge leads to confusion, and that's another major cause of mistakes.

CONFUSION

Some people become flustered and confused by the size and complexity of their task. They tend to make a lot of mistakes because they're unable – or unwilling – to take time to sort out the options that are available to them.

Instead of figuring out which option holds the greatest promise, they proceed by trial and error and take a stab at anything that strikes their fancy. They waste a lot of valuable time and resources. Because whenever they make an error, they have to start over again from scratch.

If you want to see some classic examples of mistakes caused by confusion, watch someone try to put together a child's swing set without looking at the directions, or try to organize a family reunion without knowing who all the relatives are.

People have a much better chance of being successful if they know what they want to accomplish, how they are going to accomplish it, and what they are willing to risk to do it. That's true for every task, no matter if it's trying to satisfy a lifetime goal or finish a simple errand.

Even when people know what they're supposed to do, they can still make mistakes by not using common sense.

POOR JUDGMENT

Many people make mistakes because they misjudge their own character and ability, or the character and ability of someone else. They think they can do things they can't, or they expect others to do things that are impossible.

Anyone who has entered middle age knows the effect poor judgment can have, especially if they've ever tried to play competitive tennis with a teenager.

People who exercise poor judgment are not necessarily confused about their tasks. They just misjudge the results they're going to get.

Some college students, after putting in long hours of studying, think they've been double-crossed when they find out that their exams contained all the wrong questions. It's hard for them to admit that they used poor judgment in deciding what to study.

It's easy for someone to misjudge a situation and make a mistake when they're distracted by a variety of options.

DISTRACTIONS

Mistakes commonly occur when people are forced to divide their attention among several different pursuits. By spreading themselves too thin, they expose themselves to hazards and perils that seem to come out of nowhere and clobber them when they least expect it.

A den mother who is trying to ride herd on a station wagon full of cub scouts is a good example of someone who is exposed to a lot of noisy distractions. She is also a prime candidate for a serious auto accident.

People can avoid troublesome distractions by focusing on a pre-established, mental checklist of things to do and by concentrating their efforts on tasks that pose the greatest chance for error. Otherwise they'll make more mistakes than they ever thought were possible.

They can also make a lot of mistakes when they fail to see what lies ahead.

LACK OF FORESIGHT

Mark Twain said, "It is easier to stay out than get out."

People who fail to recognize potential hazards ahead of time run the risk of suddenly getting stonewalled. By the time they realize they're in trouble, they're in too deep and have already made too many mistakes.

But be careful with this, because recognizing the possibility of error and taking steps to avoid it is not the same as saying that mistakes are going to happen.

Mountaineers don't expect to fall off the mountain when they start climbing. But they know the possibility exists, so they take every precaution to make sure it doesn't happen to them.

Some people are afraid to admit that mistakes are possible. Many newlyweds, for example, feel their marriages would be doomed from the start if they even *thought* they had made a mistake. That's probably one reason why more people get divorced than fall off mountains.

LACK OF VISION

Noah knew what he was doing even though it wasn't raining when he built the ark. But unlike Noah, many people fail to see the relationship between tasks they're working on in the present and the long-range goals and objectives they hope to reach in the future.

Many of life's greatest challenges are made up of lots of little tasks that have to be finished before a larger goal can be reached. If the people who are doing the smaller tasks can't see any significance in what they're doing, then the tasks aren't going to get done, and success will remain an elusive dream.

Imagine what would happen if electricians, plumbers, carpenters, and other craftsmen all worked independently without a set of blueprints to build a house. They wouldn't know what the house was supposed to look like or how it was supposed to work. If they finished at all, they would undoubtedly end up with a hodgepodge of wires, wood, and pipe.

DAYDREAMING

Mistakes often happen when people lose track of what they're doing and allow their minds to wander off into other areas. They usually end up doing something that is totally unrelated to the task at hand.

Brain cells operate whether people are aware of what's going on around them or not. Mistakes occur when undisciplined, spontaneous responses are allowed to take over a person's behavior.

People walk into rooms without knowing why they're there. They make phone calls without remembering who it is they're calling or why they want to talk to them. They make hasty judgments about important business opportunities or they fail to make any judgments at all. They react without knowing why.

Daydreaming can sometimes serve as a useful tool in creating new ideas. But it can be a major cause of mistakes if it's allowed to interfere with the business at hand.

Even if people know exactly what they're doing, they can still make mistakes if they don't pay attention to the risks involved.

UNKNOWN RISKS

People who goof up a lot tend to make one of two risk-related mistakes. They either sit on their rear ends and do nothing because they think the risks are too great, or they totally ignore the risks and run off half-cocked like Don Quixote.

The risk of making some mistakes is not hard to predict. That's because chance has a rhythm, like the flowing of tides, the migration of birds, the alternation of the seasons, and the cycle of growth and harvest. Mistakes happen when people interfere with predictable patterns and upset the rhythm of chance.

People get lost in snowstorms. They lose money when the market goes into a slump. And they get sick with the flu when the season is at its peak.

It's not blind luck that makes most people successful. They're successful because they've taught themselves to recognize and take advantage of favorable opportunities whenever they happen. They understand the ebb and flow of chance and they act when the probability of making a mistake is at its lowest. Chance helps them fulfill their aspirations because they know how to use it to their advantage.

Risk taking and success go hand in hand. People can't win lotteries if they don't purchase tickets. They can't make new friends if they stay cooped up in their homes all day. And they can't catch the golden ring if they don't ride the merry-go-round.

People can also make mistakes if they are mentally unprepared to tackle the tasks that are right in front of them.

FRAME OF MIND

Unstable emotional states, like boredom, anxiety, hostility, and frustration, not only cause an appalling amount of bad luck, they also cause a lot of mistakes. That's especially true for people who are mentally unprepared to handle the sudden twists of fate that can raise havoc with their goals and objectives.

The only way people can take advantage of rapid shifts in their environment is by being mentally and physically alert and by having the physical stamina needed to adapt to new situations.

Nowhere is this more evident than in the volatile commodities market where fortunes are won and lost in the span of minutes. Mental and physical alertness are just as necessary when trying to negotiate freeway traffic in the middle of a snowstorm.

Abilities count, but the belief that you *can* succeed will affect whether or not you *will* succeed.

Optimists feel in control of their lives. They act quickly, look for solutions, form new plans of action, and reach out for advice. Pessimists, on the other hand, think they're destined to live miserable lives. Their feelings of helplessness undermine their chances for success and bring on an unnecessary number of mistakes.

SELF-FULFILLING PROPHECIES

One guaranteed way for people to screw up is for them to believe they're going to make a mistake before they even start out.

Some people are firmly convinced that they're going to drop the ball and do something wrong. And because they've convinced themselves that they're going to make a mistake, they consciously, or unconsciously, make sure it actually happens. When called to task for their blunders, they usually respond by saying, "I told you so."

Many of these self-indulgent prophets set out to make deliberate mistakes to gain attention and consolation from others. They don't have enough confidence in themselves to predict success, so they predict failure. And strange as it seems, many of them are pleased about making a correct prediction. They're not bothered at all about having made a mistake.

Prophets of doom are easy to find among students who say they're going to fail an exam, athletes who predict defeat in an upcoming game, and timid salespeople who say they're going to lose a sale. In most cases, their pessimistic predictions of failure turn out to be correct.

Other people don't dare forecast mistakes because they're deathly afraid of the consequences.

FEAR

Fear is a major influence on people's lives. It's one of the biggest obstacles to success and the subject of another book in the DO IT! Success Series, entitled *Farewell To Fear*.

Fear can cause several kinds of mistakes, including common errors of omission. Anxious students fail to show up for their final examinations and flunk their courses. Frightened job applicants fail to show up for their interviews and are rejected for employment. And occasionally, a frightened groom will abandon his bride at the front door of the church.

Fear can lead to indecisiveness, which then leads to less obvious mistakes. Doctors who worry about malpractice claims exercise undue caution in treating emergency patients. Assembly workers who worry about losing their jobs hesitate to suggest changes in production methods.

Frightened people try desperately to escape the real or imagined consequences of their actions. But their worrisome behavior has just the opposite effect. It increases their anxiety and causes even more mistakes. Frantic salespeople who are afraid of being rejected by their clients will often throw together propositions that never see the light of day.

The American author Elbert Hubbard once said, "The greatest mistake you can make in life is to always be afraid that you're going to make one." That's because the fear of making a mistake produces a high level of anxiety and a poor self-image for the person who's afraid to take any action.

Anxiety comes from worrying about what might happen in the future. People can make just as many mistakes when they worry about what they've already done in the past.

GUILT

Guilt is remorse for things done in the past. It's commonly seen in athletes who feel responsible for losing the big game, in bidders who think they lost a contract, and in drivers who blame themselves for an accident.

Guilt-ridden people think bad mistakes make bad people. They punish themselves by refusing to take credit for the good things they've done or by refusing to forgive themselves for any mistakes they think they're responsible for.

People who harbor a lot of guilt are stifled by self-reproach and a loss of self-esteem, and are unable to come up with any positive ways of moving ahead. The pervasive nature of their guilt predisposes them to make similar mistakes in the future.

Guilt is not reserved for sinners and thieves. It's a common venom that can affect anybody, at any time, and in any kind of circumstance. When combined with the pressures of normal day-to-day living, it serves as a significant cause of error.

People sometimes get so involved in what they're doing that they unwittingly trap themselves into making a series of major mistakes.

ENTRAPMENT

More people would succeed in small things if they were not troubled by great ambitions. Many are lured by their egos into situations where the potential for mistakes is already well established. They're so wrapped up in their dreams and aspirations that they fail to see the dangers around them and are unable to get out before the roof caves in.

President Lincoln offered this advice for people who tend to get in over their heads. "When you have got an elephant by the hind legs, and he is trying to run away, it is best to let him run."

There is a fine art to knowing when to quit and not many people are blessed with it. Projects become so symbolic of deep-seated desires, that pulling the plug on them becomes unthinkable. Most people get trapped at the point where they have to choose between giving up or continuing. By allowing their momentum to overwhelm their judgment, they sink further and further into a losing cause. The gossamer rewards that loom ahead blot out the losses that have piled up behind.

Entrapment involves an escalating commitment and a tendency to throw more and more resources into projects that many sideline observers think are headed straight down the tube.

Shaky marriages provide classic examples of entrapment. So do many business ventures. Even hanging on to the old family station wagon long after it should be junked can result in costly repairs that could have been avoided.

People can usually save themselves from entrapment by seeking outside advice and consultation about their projects. But if they try to do everything themselves, they run the risk of making even more mistakes.

GOING IT ALONE

People who refuse to seek help from others generally act first, think afterward, and then kick themselves for not checking out the terrain ahead of time.

The English poet Alexander Pope recognized this trait years ago. His observation that "fools rush in where angels fear to tread," later became a popular song title.

Boldness is a positive attribute, but only after goals and objectives have been determined and a plan of action has been established. Uninformed boldness that is blind to danger usually proves to be disastrous. A classic example is General George Custer's bloody outing at the Battle of the Little Big Horn.

Some people who try to do everything themselves could care less about what happens when they're done. That attitude is another source of error.

LACK OF RESPONSIBILITY

People who refuse to hold themselves accountable for their actions are prime candidates for big mistakes. Their lack of responsibility and "I don't care" attitude promotes sloppiness, inefficiency, and haphazard performance.

Lack of responsibility is usually accompanied by an unwillingness to take corrective action and a refusal to help others when mistakes become apparent.

Like rats leaving a sinking ship, politicians have been known to abandon their leadership responsibilities when they see that it's politically expedient to do so. Defiant workers will sacrifice quality for expediency if they refuse to accept the terms of their negotiated labor agreement. And some employees who think they're in dead-end jobs will kiss their responsibilities goodbye, then bide their time until retirement.

Lack of responsibility is like an insidious disease. It can easily spread to others who think they are unjustly carrying the load for the malcontents. Mistakes become the rule rather than the exception as more and more people back off from their responsibilities.

Mistakes are also the rule for people who have never developed the habit of being successful.

BAD HABITS

Some people get so wrapped up in compulsive behavior patterns that they have no chance at all of reaching their goals and objectives.

Merchants lose sales because they habitually interrupt their customers instead of listening to what they have to say. Students consistently fail exams because they're in the habit of missing classes, ignoring assignments, and refusing to study. Drivers keep getting tickets because of their habitual failure to put money in parking meters.

Developing good habits and eliminating bad habits takes willpower and determination, but that's hard for many people to do. That prompted American author and advertising executive Bruce Barton to make this observation. "What a curious phenomenon it is," he said, "that you can get men to die for the liberty of the world who will not make the little sacrifice that is needed to free themselves from their own individual bondage."

COMING UP

By now, you should have a pretty good idea of why people make mistakes. It's possible that some of the causes you just read about were on the list you made back on page 12. When you add them all together, you should be able to come up with some pretty good ideas for staying out of trouble.

Latch on to anything you think might be useful right away. Add it to your repertoire of strategies for geting ahead. Pay particular attention to any strategies that can help you eliminate those little day-to-day mistakes that keep holding you back. If you can get rid of them, you'll be in great shape to put an end to the big mistakes that keep you from reaching your long-range goals and objectives.

Pause for a minute now to catch your breath. Then reflect back on everything you've read so far. Add a little fire to your commitment to being error-free. Turn up the front burner and get some optimism cooking. Then move on to Section III and find out what you need to do to work your way up the ladder of success.

HOW TO AVOID MISTAKES

There are 24 techniques in this section, and every one is designed to keep you from making mistakes. Study them closely as you compare them with what you've come up with so far. Pick out the techniques that can help you most and start using them right away. Come back to the other techniques after you've gained some confidence and started rolling up a list of successes.

These are general-purpose techniques. You can apply them to your normal day-to-day errands and tasks or to your long-term goals and objectives. Be sure to focus in on specific problem areas so you won't go running off in a dozen different directions.

Add to your list of techniques as you go along. Keep trying to do better. Remember that your primary goal is to reduce the probability of making a mistake and increase the probability of being successful.

The first technique is probably the most important.

KNOW WHERE YOU'RE GOING

Turn to page 24 and write down, as clearly as you can, the main things you want out of life and what you have to do to get them. List your long-term goals along with your short-range objectives. Put down special projects that you've been meaning to finish. Then, before you begin a task that's on the list, tell yourself exactly what you want to do and what you want to accomplish by doing it.

Be precise, because if you don't know where you're going, you'll probably end up somewhere else.

WHAT I WANT OUT OF LIFE AND
WHAT I HAVE TO DO TO BE SUCCESSFUL

Write down what you have to do to reach your goals and objectives.

My long-term goals _____

_____

_____

_____

Long-term tasks I have to complete _____

_____

_____

_____

My short-range objectives _____

_____

_____

_____

Short-range tasks I have to complete _____

_____

_____

_____

Be distinct. Don't confuse meaningful, well-defined goals and objectives with tentative, wishy-washy aspirations that have little or no substance.

Be decisive. Stick to your own private blend of desires. Don't settle for what others want, or for what others think you should be doing. Set your own sails and write down wants, needs, and desires that are important to you.

Be realistic. It's better to be on the lookout for modest rewards than to be sustained by an illusion of enormous riches.

As soon as you know where you're going, you'll have to find out everything you can about how to get there.

GET THE FACTS

Learn everything you can about the goals and objectives you're trying to reach. Look for special requirements and unique characteristics of the tasks you're trying to accomplish. Be ready to apply new knowledge where it will do the most good.

If you're after a college degree, know what courses you have to take to fulfill your requirements. If you want to be financially independent, read books on investing. If you're driving to a strange destination, check a map before you begin your journey.

It's easy to learn something about everything, but it's very difficult to learn everything about one single subject. So don't try to get by on what you already know. That's probably very little compared to everything else there is to be learned.

You'll know soon enough if there are gaps in your knowledge by how well you're able to get through the material you're trying to learn.

Spend extra time in areas that give you the most difficulty since those will be the ones that will harbor the most mistakes.

Anticipate your need for knowledge. It will give you a headstart on filling in any empty spaces. Scrounge up new sources of information, and squeeze out of them as much as you possibly can. Use your mind to create spinoffs where gaps occur. Cultivate new knowldege from old. Ask questions.

An investment in new knowledge always pays the best interest. The only expense involved is time. If you didn't spend time on learning, it would probably be lost on your mistakes.

You won't lose time and you won't make many mistakes if you stick with what you're good at and like to do.

BUILD ON YOUR STRENGTHS

Stop for a minute and take inventory of your strengths and weaknesses. Make an honest appraisal of what you can and cannot do.

Focus on specific areas of strength like skills, talents, experience, intelligence, motivation, and personal appearance. Don't forget to add things you've done in the past that have given you a lot of satisfaction and have earned you praise and recognition from other people. Put down things you really get a kick out of doing.

Take a long, hard look at your weaknesses. Put down personal and professional activities that you're not very good at. Include things you don't like to do, or would like to avoid if at all possible; things like getting up early, speaking in public, or writing a detailed report.

Compare your lists of strengths and weaknesses with the list of goals and objectives that you made on page 24. Ask yourself if you're doing things you're good at and like to do and avoiding things you're not good at and don't like to do. That's what you should be doing, because that will bring you the most success and result in the fewest mistakes.

Don't agonize over a lack of skills. If you find something missing and want to acquire it, take time to learn it. If you can't acquire it, do the best you can with the skills you've got. Just don't try to do something for which you are totally unprepared, or you'll set yourself up for some colossal blunders.

You have a much better chance of avoiding mistakes altogether if you spend your time doing things that have a high priority.

SET PRIORITIES

You live in a competitive, success-oriented society where money, possessions, and a good physique are highly regarded. Test your values in that environment. Then decide what you really want out of life and what you have to do to be successful at it.

Turn back to page 24 and rank your goals and objectives according

MY LIST OF STRENGTHS

Make a list of things you're good at and like to do.

_____

_____

_____

_____

_____

_____

_____

_____

_____

_____

_____

_____

_____

_____

_____

_____

_____

_____

_____

MY LIST OF WEAKNESSES

Make a list of things you're not good at and don't like to do.

_____

_____

_____

_____

_____

_____

_____

_____

_____

_____

_____

_____

_____

to their urgency and importance. Put essential tasks at the top of your list and secondary ones at the bottom. You're bound to be successful if you concentrate on the essential, high-priority activities and pursue them vigorously.

Decide which tasks are important and which are urgent. Come to terms with the tasks you have to do right away and those that can be done later. Know the order in which certain milestones have to be met before you can move on to other areas. Don't run for home until you've touched all the bases.

Reevaluate your priorities from time to time. Make sure you are homing in on tasks that will keep you on track and moving in the right direction. And be sure to keep your eyes peeled on the road ahead so you don't run into any unexpected obstacles.

KNOW WHAT TO EXPECT

Anyone can make a mistake at anytime. But you can greatly reduce the probability of that mistake happening to you if you're physically and mentally alert. Learn what you can about the potential for errors, and work out contingency plans.

Look for obstacles that can cause frustration. See where they lie in wait, and figure out what you have to do to remove them, ignore them, or go around them.

Use your imagination. Picture opportunities and obstacles in your mind's eye as clearly as possible before you encounter them. Prepare to deal with them ahead of time, even though they may never come your way.

Simple preparation, like learning everything you can about some anticipated event, will keep you alert and motivated until the actual event takes place.

Another way of avoiding mistakes is by accepting responsibility for the way you carry out your tasks and activities.

BE RESPONSIBLE

Being responsibile means knowing what has to be done, doing it the best way you know how, and accepting the consequences for doing it the way you did.

You're the architect of your destiny. You should be willing to answer for your behavior and to abide by the outcomes—whether good or bad—for whatever you do.

Responsibility is not measured according to how much you lose when you screw up. It's measured according to how good you are at making the right decisions and how willing you are to accept the consequences when things don't turn out the way you want them to.

If you decide that something is worth doing, then it's worth doing right. Dedicate your efforts to that notion, even when you think it won't matter. If you only apply yourself when you feel like it, you'll open the door to a whole raft of mistakes.

Listen and be responsive to criticism. Show your critics that you've heard what's been said. Share the blame when the going gets rough. It's the tax you have to pay for being successful. Accept what you must, learn what you can, and move on.

MINIMIZE YOUR RISKS

Separate common tasks from uncommon ones. Look for tasks you haven't done before. Identify them with distinctive names so you won't get confused about what you're supposed to be working on. Form mental pictures of successful outcomes, then highlight them with unique labels.

Use common, time-tested procedures for run-of-the-mill tasks, but be creative when you have to complete unusual ones. Accentuate unique aspects of your tasks, and give them special attention.

Meeting your spouse at the airport is a lot different than meeting the King of Norway. Recognize the differences and be prepared to handle them in appropriate ways.

Subdivide large tasks into smaller ones, then attack them one by one. The enthusiasm you'll experience in completing the subtasks will speed you toward your overall goal and give you a tremendous sense of accomplishment. You'll discover what Leo Hauser has said many times. "By the yard it's hard, by the inch it's a cinch."

Make strange tasks familiar. Get to know all the parts of your tasks before you start working on them. Discover the relationships that exists between unique and common elements and use those connections to your advantage.

Use environmental cues. Park your car against the garage wall so you can see if your headlights are still on. Leave your car keys on top of the outgoing mail so you won't forget to drop off your letters at the post office.

Keep your mind sharp and uncluttered. Don't let unrelated thoughts keep you from concentrating on the task at hand. Face distractions head on and move them out of your way. Resolve the argument with your roommate before you head for class. Or at least clarify the issues so you don't spend all day stewing over a misunderstanding.

Spread your risk to others. Delegate whenever you can, especially to those who are more skilled than you. They'll help you get your tasks done, and they'll be less critical of the outcome.

You'll be less critical too if you can keep thinking positive thoughts about what you're doing.

THINK POSITIVELY

Scientific studies have shown that optimism can help a person be happier, healthier, and more successful. Pessimism, on the other hand will lead to hopelessness, sickness, and failure.

There's power in positive thinking. If you believe strongly that you have what it takes to be successful, you will have it. If you don't believe you have it, you won't get it in a million years.

The key to success is to stay in control, especially when it looks like things are starting to fall apart. Act quickly, reach out for advice, look for a lasting solution, and form a new plan of action. If you assume that nothing can be done, your assumption will result in failure.

Act confidently and you'll gain confidence. Every crisis will become an opportunity; a situation in which you can gain something new, prove yourself, do well, and succeed.

Remember that you don't have to get an "A" in everything you do. The person who finishes last in medical school is still called "doctor".

Renew the commitment to succeed that you made earlier. Strengthen it by giving yourself credit when credit is due. Acknowledge all the big and little successes you've earned along the way. Reinforce your belief that you can eliminate mistakes as easily as anyone else.

Positive thoughts will build your confidence and help you overcome fear.

OVERCOME FEAR

Common mistakes should humble you, not frighten you.

Think of the worst possible thing that could happen to you if you continued on course. Write it down on a piece of paper so you know exactly what you're afraid of. It could be failing in business, getting a divorce, smashing up your car, flunking out of school, or forgetting to send back your Reader's Digest sweepstakes form.

Assume for a moment that this menacing catastrophe is actually going to happen. Take another piece of paper and write down as many solutions to your worst fear as you can think of. Improvise if you have to, but be sure the things you put down are really going to work.

Focus on the one solution that you think would help the most to solve the problem and eliminate your fear. Get a good, clear picture of that solution in your mind.

Take a positive attitude and think of positive results. Send out your resume. Schedule a job interview. See a counselor. Enroll in a self-improvement class.

Now that you've faced your worst fear, leave it behind. Get a little success under your belt, build your confidence, and before you know it, the rest of your fears will melt like morning mist.

POSITION YOURSELF

"The secret of success in life," said the English statesman Benjamin Disraeli, "is for a man to be ready for his opportunity when it comes."

If you're in position to recognize favorable chances and extract good luck from them, you'll minimize the probability of making a mistake and maximize the probability of being successful.

Francis Bacon, the Engligh philospher, added another dimension to Disraeli's axiom. "A wise man," he said, "will make more opportunities than he finds."

You can't sell products if you don't meet customers. You can't make a passing grade if you never go to class. And you can't make new friends if you don't get out and meet people.

You can increase the number of opportunities available to you by maintaining warm, friendly relationships with everyone you meet. The more things other people know about you, the more likely they'll be to remember facts or think of ideas that will increase your chances of success.

You'll also increase your chances of success by keeping your goals and objectives clearly in sight.

VISUALIZE

You can do anything faster and better if you can see yourself getting it done. The key lies in the intensity of your vision and the depth of your concentration. All it takes is preparation, concentration, and a vivid imagination.

Determine ahead of time what steps you're going to take to reach your goal. Concentrate on milestones and subtasks. Focus on opportunities and challenges. Come up with unique solutions to recognizable problems. Use your imagination and the power of suggestion to visualize in your mind's eye a realistic expectation of what lies ahead.

Create a vivid image of yourself as a triumphant personality striding toward far horizons of constructive achievement. Picture yourself overcoming obstacles, meeting deadlines, and being successful without making a single mistake.

Use visual cues whenever you can. Collect pictures of other people who have reached the same goals you're aspiring to. See yourself in their shoes whenever your confidence begins to sag.

If you're striving for an advanced position, print the job title on a card and paste it on the refrigerator door where you'll see it every day.

Try anything, as long as it preserves your vision of success. If you find something that works, hang on to it. Modify it as your goals change, but don't lose its visionary powers.

APPRECIATE TIME

Lost wealth can be restored through hard work. Lost health can generally be regained through good living. But lost time is gone forever, so don't waste it. Budget time as you would any other scarce and valuable resource.

The time you have available for any activity will determine the odds of your making a mistake while doing it. The more time you have, the fewer errors you'll make.

But as Charles Buxton, the English author said, "You will never find time for anything. If you want time, you must make it."

Be realistic in your time estimates. Don't try to do more than is humanly possible in the time that's available, and don't try unnecessary shortcuts. Resist the urge to combine activities in an attempt to save time. Plan your strategy in advance if you see any obstacles or time constraints lying in your path.

Try to strike a balance between the time you spend on long-term tasks and time you spend on tasks that can be done in very short periods. Allow for unexpected events that can steal time and increase your chance of making a mistake. Make every minute count.

Recognize seasons and cycles, and schedule your projects according to a calendar. Income tax returns are always due in April, so start getting ready in March. Christmas always comes in December, so start shopping in November. Final exams always come at the end of a term, so start studying after the first day of class.

Once you learn how to budget your time, apply it to a plan for getting things done. Follow the lead of people—like you—who can't afford to make mistakes.

DEVELOP A GAME PLAN

Seasoned explorers never start off on a trek without a detailed itinerary. Commercial airline pilots never leave the gate without filing detailed flight plans. Even the kid who delivers your newspaper has a route to follow.

Know what you're going to do, when you're going to do it, and where it will take you once you're finished. Define your objectives early. Explore available options. Weigh advantages and disadvantages, and proceed without hesitation according to a workable plan.

Identify progressive milestones that will keep you on track and help mark your progress. Develop subgoals that can be reached in relatively short periods of time. But avoid being taken in by meaningless, short-term solutions that can cause you to lose sight of your long-term goals.

Former U.C.L.A. basketball coach John Wooden believed that "failing to prepare is preparing to fail." That philosophy made him one of the most successful coaches of all time. It can probably do as much for you if you use it.

Once you've developed a workable game plan, commit it to memory so it becomes automatic. Then all you have to worry about is how you're going to put it into effect.

KNOW WHERE TO START

"Our grand business is not to see what lies dimly in the distance but to do what lies clearly at hand."

As the words of the English philosopher Thomas Carlyle suggest, most projects follow a definite sequence in which one task has to be done before another can be attempted. The key to the successful completion of those tasks is knowing what the order is and following it.

Test yourself as you meet new challenges along the way. If you find you're on the wrong track, stop. Then get back on the right track and start over again.

Different people start in different ways as you can see by watching people swim. Some will dive right in and others will ease in slowly while trying to adjust to the temperature of the water. There's no right or wrong way to go swimming. But there are some things that everyone has to know. You have to know how to swim, you have to know how deep the water is, and you have to know if there are any rocks, broken bottles, or sea-monsters lurking beneath the surface.

It shouldn't surprise you to know that there is a right way to do everything, from how to stay happily married to how to install a faucet. And it always helps to read or listen to someone else's directions before you start. If you were to check your local library or bookstore, you could probably find a how-to-do-it book that deals with your specific goals and objectives.

Once you've figured out how to start your project, you have to come up with a sensible way of proceeding with it.

DO ONE THING AT A TIME

If you try to do two things at the same time, you'll run the risk of doing neither.

Set aside, for a moment, all the other things you have to do and direct your attention to the single, most important task at hand. When you've exhausted your attention on that task, shift to another and give that one your best shot. Just be sure you're moving ahead and not backwards, off to the side, or flat on your face.

If you're overwhelmed by the size of your task, remember what was said earlier. Subdivide it into smaller parts and work on one part at a time. You'll reduce the risk of error, and you'll be exposed to smaller doses of frustration. You'll also experience a greater sense of accomplishment, which will add encouragement to your overall effort and motivate you to do more.

Avoid distractions when you're in the middle of a critical task. Tell yourself, and others, that you can't leave what you're doing to take on something else. If an interruption is unavoidable, be sure to remember where you left off so you can come back to the right spot. Then continue with your task until you're finished.

RUN TO DAYLIGHT

Find a way or make one. If you come up against a major obstacle, stop. Gather up your strategies for being successful, look for another path that is leading in the right direction, and then run to daylight. Take advantage of life's rapid shifts, but stay on track.

Don't get discouraged if you find yourself in uncharted territory. The first of the new is always harder than the last of the highly developed old. Just keep doing what you're good at and before you know it, you'll be back in familiar territory.

Expect anything and be alert for everything, especially favorable opportunities. They generally have the power to offset a run of bad luck, and they can propel you toward your goal with surprising accuracy.

Be prepared to make adjustments in your overall game plan at the first sign of a threatening obstacle. Approach every situation as if it were a question to be answered, not a problem to be solved.

GO STEADILY INTO THE WIND

Hang on to the tiller, no matter which way the wind blows. You only fail if you fail to try.

Throw your mind outward, away from fears and misgivings, and let it focus on the external realities that control your hopes and aspirations. Push beyond the present and into the future.

The indisputable law of the universe is progress. What you gain in one activity is invested in everything that follows. So keep your purpose constantly in sight and know where life is taking you.

The zestful pursuit of your goals and objectives will keep you from going stale, help stimulate your hopes for success, and reduce your chances of making a mistake.

Increase your capacity to endure in the face of adversity by eliminating fear and negative thoughts. Be persistent. Staying power is not blind adherence to a lost cause, it's the courageous pursuit of an attainable goal.

Staying power generates energy and renews enthusiasm. But you have to follow through with it to make it last, because persistence that results in one success doesn't always guarantee an equally triumphant sequel.

Knowing when to push ahead is an effective way of avoiding mistakes. But so is knowing when to back off.

KNOW WHEN TO QUIT

Anyone can make a mistake, but only a knucklehead will continue to make the same mistake over and over again.

If you're still making mistakes after you've done everything you can on a project, then it's time to call it quits.

Quitting is not a sign of personal failure. It takes courage and strength of character, especially after you've invested a lot of valuable time and energy in your efforts.

Base your decision to stay or quit on what the future has to offer, not on how much you've given up in the past. Set your ego aside without bruising your self-confidence. Downplay the significance of winning, especially if the cards are stacked against you.

Put a limit on your losses. Redefine your goals and objectives if they seem out of reach, then pursue them with new resolve.

KEEP A JOURNAL

It's a lot easier to recognize the mistakes of others than to remember your own. That's why it's important to keep a journal.

A journal is a day-to-day accounting of ideas, events, reflections, and experiences. It's something you keep on a regular basis for your own personal use. It helps you see what worked in the past and what didn't. Its history of emotional responses tells you how you reacted to a variety of obstacles and opportunities.

American author Ralph Waldo Emerson said, "The years teach us what the days never knew." That's the beauty of keeping a journal. Over the long haul it will tell you what you've done in the past, show you where you are in the present, and help you chart a course for the future.

Use your journal to monitor how well you're doing in your pursuit of success. Study your wins and losses and write down, unedited and uncensored, the first thing that comes to mind. Look for causes and explanations. Validate your strategies so you can avoid your mistakes and duplicate your successes.

Don't get discouraged by temporary setbacks. And above all, don't feel guilty if things go wrong.

AVOID GUILT

What you have done cannot be undone. It can only be done over again or forgotten. The past cannot be changed. What you do in the future is still within your power.

Own up to your mistakes through honest self-assessment. It's another way of saying you are wiser today than you were yesterday.

Don't try to explain or excuse your errors through punishing self-criticism. And don't use the nature and size of your screwups as a gauge for the amount of guilt you're going to feel.

Protect your self-esteem from self-destruction. Fix briefly what can be fixed and apologize briefly for what can't. Acknowledge the cause of the mistake, then get on with the rest of your life.

Don't waste time dwelling on past errors. You'll get run over by forward-looking people who have their sights set on success.

Face your critics head on. Keep everything out in front so no one can misinterpret what you're doing. Track down rumors and put them to rest. If you can't do anymore than say you're sorry, then do it, and walk away. Ignore people who want to hold a grudge against you. But don't ignore those who can help you gain additional knowledge.

SHARE WITH OTHERS

"From the errors of others a wise man corrects his own."

The words of Publius Syrus, the Roman slave and poet, suggest that honest mistakes generate a need for support and reassurance. When you share your experiences with others, you'll find that someone else has probably made the same mistakes you've made or are trying to avoid. And the mistakes you've already made are no worse than the ones they're trying to forget.

Look for role models as a source of inspiration and encouragement. Talk to those who have successfully negotiated the pathways you're on now. Learn from their experiences and avoid their mistakes. Duplicate their successes whenever you can.

Look for objective opinions and advice. Ignore people who resent your attempts to do the things they should be doing, like getting rid of bad habits and destructive life styles. Their criticism and lack of courage is generally spawned by jealousy.

One of the best tests of a friendship is for one friend to point out another's mistakes. It's better to get a little chiding from a friend than to bear the hostility of a stranger. No one likes to hear criticism, but by and large, it's a lot more useful than praise. Listen to your spouse, children, friends, and colleagues. Seek their advice and welcome their encouragement.

Your strength as an individual will depend on how well you react to criticism and praise.

REWARD YOURSELF

There are more people who know how to win than there are those who know how to make proper use of their victories.

Success comes when you realize that your preparation resulted in a satisfactory solution. For that you should be rewarded.

Self-rewards maintain self-esteem. Self-esteem breeds optimism and self-control. And a sense of control is an excellent indicator of future and continued success. If you accepted only the evaluations of others as being the total truth, you'd be allowing others to dictate who you are.

Set up personal incentives and reward yourself when you reach your goals.

Rewards can be simple and inexpensive. But they should be things that are important to you. A bottle of wine, a hot-fudge sundae, a night on the town, or a long-overdue vacation can all help maintain your confidence and motivation.

Reward yourself only when you've earned it. But if you've earned a reward, be sure to take it. A reward system only works when you stick with it. It might even become habit-forming.

MAKE SUCCESS A HABIT

Success will become automatic once you get in the habit of doing things right. Start with common, everyday tasks that have given you fits in the past. Pay your bills on time, stay below the speed limit, remember birthdays and anniversaries, and complete class or work assignments before they're due.

Make an initial list of tasks you're going to tackle and decide what steps you need to take to bring them to a successful conclusion. Practice those steps until they're easy. When they're easy, you'll begin to enjoy them. When you start enjoying them, you'll do them more often. And finally, you'll do them so often that they'll become second nature.

Make up your mind that you're going to be successful. Experiment to find the best, easiest, and quickest way of getting things done. Set aside specific times for developing successful habits. Monitor your behavior from time to time to make sure you're on the right track.

The best way to train your mind and develop good habits is to do it on your own initiative. Others may help you, guide you, and inspire you. But the things that will help the most to ensure success are the results you get through your own efforts. Whatever you get out of any undertaking is always directly related to the effort you put in.

If you want to get rid of a bad habit, like making mistakes, you first have to dislike it. You have to resent it with enough intensity to generate the energy and determination needed to replace it with a habit you enjoy, like being successful.

Put all thoughts of failure out of your mind. Just remember that the only water that will sink a ship is water that gets inside it.

CARE ENOUGH TO DO YOUR VERY BEST

James Bryant Conant, the famous American educator, said that "each honest calling, each walk of life, has its own elite, its own aristocracy based on excellence."

Wil Bernthal, a well-known management professor at the University of Colorado, often talked about "doing an uncommon job uncommonly well."

It's what Henry Wadsworth Longfellow recognized as "doing what you do well and doing well whatever you do."

Success is not reserved for the rich and famous. Nor is it always based on skill. You'll find error-free performances among farmers as well as physicians, among secretaries as well as scientists, and among bricklayers as well as bankers. Skill is only one component of success. The main ingredient is attitude.

If you were to make a checklist of successful attitudes, you'd have to include joy, love, poise, faith, courage, patience, honesty, confidence, tolerance, cheerfulness, humility, serenity, optimism, initiative, enthusiasm, imagination, and last but not least, personal pride.

One way of developing a successful attitude is to use the well-known technique of the French psychotherapist Emile Coue. He advised his patients to face themselves in the mirror every morning and repeat several times, "Every day, in every way, I'm getting better and better."

Once you've developed the right attitudes, the next step is to develop a workable plan of action. That's the subject of the final section.

YOUR PLAN OF ACTION

You've gotten this far in life, so you must be doing a lot of things right. Now it's time to expand your expectations for the future by allowing your attitudes to reflect the successful experiences of your past.

Error-free living is not impossible. Success is not a pipe dream.

This book has helped you gain a better idea of why you make mistakes. And it has given you all the basic ingredients for a successful plan of action. Now all you have to do is add a hefty dose of optimism, mix it all together, and apply it where it will do the most good.

Give it your best shot and don't worry about coming up short. Even if you miss the first time out you'll still have the satisfaction of knowing that you gave it everything you had. And don't worry about making more mistakes, because next time you'll know what to do to avoid them.

Be persistent. Every day presents a brandnew opportunity to grow and be happy, so take advantage of it. Develop a winning attitude and believe in your ability to pull off the unbelievable.

Concentrate on what you're doing, not what you did. If you try to uncover the source of every error, you'll get distracted and your dreams of the future will vanish into thin air. If the lion gets out of its cage, try to figure out how you're going to get it back in. Don't sit and wonder how it got out or you'll be eaten alive.

"Success is never final." said Winston Churchill. "If you don't progress, you'll stagnate."

Even if you were perched on the loftiest throne in the world, you'd still be sitting on your behind.

Prime the pump, and do it now. If you wait until you're in the mood, you may wait forever.

And if someone tells you you're crazy for trying to eliminate all of your mistakes, just tell them to get in the back of the pack behind you and Roger Bannister.

INDEX

INDEX

—Notes—

—Notes—

—Notes—

—Notes—